THE **COCK TAVERN** THEATRE

Formed in January 2009, under the artistic leadership of Adam Spreadbury-Maher, The Cock Tavern Theatre runs a dangerous programme of new writing and critical revivals by the world's most challenging playwrights. It established itself at the forefront of the London Fringe within its first year by winning the prestigious *'Dan Crawford Pub Theatre Award'* at the Peter Brook Empty Space Awards 2009. The Cock Tavern Theatre has premiered work by Tennessee Williams, Edward Bond, Hannie Rayson and Jack Hibberd, and staged crucial revivals by Nick Ward, Adrian Pagan, Louis Nowra, Stephen Fry and Jon Fosse. In 2010 Adam Spreadbury-Maher was awarded *'Best Artistic Director'* at the Fringe Report Awards. In April 2010 The Cock Tavern Theatre became a producing venue for resident companies Good Night Out Presents and OperaUpClose. For six months it was home to the record-breaking Olivier Award winning *La Bohème*, which has twice transferred to Soho Theatre and joins the repertory programme at London's Little Opera House (at the King's Head Theatre). In March and April 2011 The Cock Tavern Theatre produced two Tennessee Williams world premieres to celebrate the playwright's 100th birthday.

Artistic Director: Adam Spreadbury-Maher
Executive Director: Ben Cooper
Executive Producer: Dominic Haddock
Programme Manager: Roxanne Peak-Payne
Theatre Manager: Kate Mara
Press and Marketing Manager: Nathan Godkin
Assistant to the Directors: Kat Ould
Associate Director: Hamish MacDougall
Literary Associate: Robyn Winfield-Smith
International Literary Associate: Tanja Pagnuco

T0353294

To Mum and Dad

Rob Hayes

A BUTCHER OF DISTINCTION

OBERON BOOKS
LONDON

First published in 2011 by Oberon Books Ltd
521 Caledonian Road, London N7 9RH
Tel: 020 7607 3637 / Fax: 020 7607 3629
e-mail: info@oberonbooks.com
www.oberonbooks.com

A catalogue record for this book is available from the British Library.

ISBN: 978-1-84943-030-2

Cover image Maureen Price

Acknowledgements

Special thanks to Ned, Sam, Ciaràn, Michael, Lewis, Fi, Kate, Fay, Caitlin, Adam, and the inhabitants and associates of Ladcom Street.

A Butcher of Distinction was first performed at The Cock Tavern Theatre, London on the 3rd April 2011 with following cast:

TEDDY, Michael Gould
HARTLEY, Ciaran Owens
HUGO, Sam Swann

Director, Ned Bennett
Assistant Director, Lewis Hayes
Designer, Fiona Russell
Sound, Peter Eltringham
Lighting Designer, Joshua Carr
Producer, Adam Spreadbury-Maher and Caitlin Albery-Beavan
Production Manager, Kate Mara

SCENE ONE

A Pub basement. Dank. It has been turned into a makeshift living space. The odd piece of furniture stands amongst piles of junk and debris. Every surface is littered with boxes, bags, random objects or stacks of papers. Everything is tatty and old.

HUGO stands with two large boxes at his feet. He is holding an old hair dryer. HARTLEY is distracted, trying to set fire to a ream of documents with a lighter.

HUGO: So he lived here then.

HARTLEY turns to HUGO, sees the hair dryer.

HARTLEY: Sell it.

HUGO drops it into a box and picks up a neck brace.

HUGO: That man who let us in.

HARTLEY: Sell that.

HUGO drops it into a box and picks up a novelty shoehorn.

HUGO: Hartley, the man who let us in.

HARTLEY: Sell it. What about him?

HUGO: Do you think he was daddy's friend?

HUGO picks up a bottle of ether.

HARTLEY: What's that?

HUGO: I don't know. Ether.

Beat.

HARTLEY: Sell it.

HUGO: Hartley.

HARTLEY: I doubt it.

HUGO drops it into a box.

HUGO: Why?

HARTLEY: He was quite...

HARTLEY waves a hand over his face.

HARTLEY: Dusky.

HUGO: Yes, he was rather.

HARTLEY: Remember what daddy used to say about Indians.

HUGO: Drown them.

HUGO looks to the box at his feet. It is overflowing.

HUGO: We're going to need another sell box.

HARTLEY: Give it a shake. It might settle.

HUGO: It's full.

HARTLEY: Do we have anything in the keep box?

HUGO: A bottle of Prosecco.

HARTLEY: Prosecco...

HUGO: You said it might appreciate in value.

HARTLEY: We'll take the hit on the Prosecco. Get rid of it and we'll use the keep box for any overspill.

HUGO takes out a bottle of Prosecco from the box and puts it on the floor.

HUGO: Do we need a new keep box?

HARTLEY: Let's worry about that when we have something to keep.

HUGO: There's a lot of them round here isn't there?

HARTLEY: What?

HUGO: Of those kinds of people.

HARTLEY: What's your point?

HUGO: Interesting that daddy would choose to stay here. Considering his views on...what did he call it?

HARTLEY: Repatriation.

HUGO picks up a box, has trouble opening it.

HUGO: I think it's interesting.

HARTLEY: It's not.

HUGO rips open the box, several bottles of prescription medication fall out.

HARTLEY: What's that?

HUGO picks up a bottle, reads the label. HARTLEY snatches it off him and reads the label himself.

He shakes it next to his ear, then tosses it into the sell box.

HARTLEY: Sell.

HUGO: What is it?

HARTLEY: I said sell.

HUGO: All of it?

HARTLEY: Yes Hugo.

HUGO collects the bottles and puts them in the sell box. He picks up another object.

HUGO: Smells a bit in here.

Beat.

HUGO: Hartley.

HARTLEY: All the more reason to hurry up then.

HUGO picks up a tie. He drops it into the box. HARTLEY runs over and takes it out.

HARTLEY: What did I say?

HUGO: What? About what?

HARTLEY: The crest.

HUGO: Crest?

HARTLEY: Anything with the family crest on it. Do you know what it looks like? With the lions...?

HARTLEY holds the tie up for HUGO to see.

HUGO: Course I know what it looks like.

HARTLEY: If you see anything with it on, give it to me.

HUGO: Right. Sorry.

HARTLEY: Just – please try and pay attention.

HUGO: Anything with the crest, give to you.

HARTLEY: It's very important.

HUGO: And everything else we sell.

HARTLEY: No – show me, and we'll make a decision.

HUGO: Together.

HARTLEY: Y – Yes.

HARTLEY turns and sees HUGO with his handkerchief.

HARTLEY: What's that?

HUGO: My handkerchief.

Beat.

HARTLEY: Sell it.

HUGO puts it back in his pocket.

HUGO: You think all this will be enough then?

HARTLEY: Enough for what?

HUGO: To keep us going. Financially.

HARTLEY: Till the money turns up, yes.

HUGO: Good. Good.

HARTLEY keeps looking.

HUGO: Smells like an armpit.

HARTLEY: We're actually in a bit of a rush old boy, so if you could...

HUGO makes an effort to keep looking.

HUGO: So, six, seven months...

HARTLEY: What?

HUGO: To find the money.

HARTLEY: About that. Maybe less.

HUGO: How much do hair dryers usually go for then?

HARTLEY: Pardon?

HUGO: Just wondering how much you think we can get for the old broken hair dryer?

HUGO: I don't know.

HUGO: What about half a bottle of Ether? Or a novelty shoe horn?

HARTLEY: We sell it as a job lot.

HUGO: With the neck brace...

HARTLEY: I'm sorry, am I sensing a tone here?

HUGO: Nope. No tone. Well one tone, but it's the normal one. The normal speaking tone.

HARTLEY: Good. Let's keep it that way.

HUGO: I'm happy if you're happy.

HARTLEY: I am happy.

HUGO: Good.

HARTLEY: I'm over the bloody moon Hugo.

HUGO: Excellent.

HARTLEY: Good. I know it looks like junk but it's –

HUGO: No, I didn't mean –

HARTLEY: But it's daddy's –

HUGO: Yeah yeah –

HARTLEY: It's all his things –

HUGO: No, yes of course.

HARTLEY: And it all adds up.

HUGO: Yes. To what though, is what I'm asking.

HARTLEY: Everything has a value. Everything.

Beat. HARTLEY refocuses his attention to HUGO.

HARTLEY: Okay, I've just boned a pig – Don't laugh. I've just boned a nice fat pig for the market.

HARTLEY picks up a gold pocket watch and holds it up.

HARTLEY: Pork shoulder. Lovely and juicy and expensive.

He drops it into the sell box and picks up a ream of copper wire.

HARTLEY: Offal.

He drops it into the sell box.

HUGO: So what's all the medication?

HARTLEY shrugs.

HARTLEY: The brain.

HUGO: No one ever buys pig brain.

HARTLEY: Someone always buys the brain. You ever had one of Mrs. Glenister's pork pies?

HUGO: I used to love them.

HARTLEY: Head cheese and ligaments. Nothing else.

HUGO pulls a face.

HARTLEY: Man cannot live on pork shoulder alone.

HUGO: You have to sell the whole pig.

HARTLEY: It all adds up.

HUGO: And what about the crest? The things with the crest?

HARTLEY: We take them with us. Every one.

HARTLEY returns to his search. HUGO picks up a lampshade for HARTLEY to inspect. HARTLEY doesn't notice.

HUGO: I'm hungry.

Beat.

HUGO: Hartley I'm hungry. Are you hungry?

HARTLEY: There's no time.

HUGO: We haven't eaten all day. I feel dizzy.

HARTLEY stands up, frustrated.

HARTLEY: Hang on.

He rifles through a nearby cupboard, takes out a packet of dried noodles.

HUGO: What is it? Can I have some?

He turns the packet over.

HUGO: What is it Hartley?

He scans the cooking instructions.

HUGO: Can I have some?

He drops the packet.

HARTLEY: We'll eat on the train, okay? We'll get a sandwich on the train home. Not long now.

HUGO: What about upstairs? They might do food.

HARTLEY: No. Absolutely not. No one must...we'll eat on the train.

HUGO nods.

HUGO: Very hungry...

HARTLEY goes back to his search.

HUGO: And if the money...

HARTLEY: What?

HUGO: Isn't...

HARTLEY: Isn't what? Out with it.

HUGO: If the money doesn't...isn't forthcoming?

HARTLEY: And what makes you think it won't be forthcoming?

HUGO: Nothing. No reason at all. I'm just asking what if.

HARTLEY: I think you've asked enough questions for the time being.

HUGO: Sorry. It's just everything's gone though.

HARTLEY: I know Hugo. Don't tell me things I already know.

HUGO: But if there was more money somewhere then he could've used that to pay his debts, rather than selling –

HARTLEY: Hugo!

HUGO: – everything we own.

HARTLEY: Where are you going with all this? What are you trying to say?

HUGO: Nothing. Just what I said, right then.

HARTLEY: What do you think he did down here the whole time? He had interests beyond rural Herefordshire you know. Just because it's hidden, doesn't mean it's not out there.

HUGO: It's hidden.

HARTLEY: Yes.

HUGO: Like a treasure chest.

HARTLEY: If you like.

HUGO: Like a treasure chest from a pirate story.

HARTLEY: Yes.

HUGO: From a made up pirate story.

HARTLEY: I beg your pardon?

HUGO: Who was he hiding it all from? If it is hidden.

HARTLEY: Okay, I'm definitely sensing a tone now.

HUGO: It's just a tone of curiosity. Bordering on slight concern.

HARTLEY: You're being annoying.

HUGO: I'm not being annoying.

HARTLEY: Well that's subjective isn't it? I'm getting annoyed by you, so you are in fact being annoying.

HUGO: Am I annoying?

HARTLEY: It's not a factual...thing – currently, at the moment, you are being annoying. It's not your permanent state or anything. Just right now...

HUGO: You're finding me annoying...

HARTLEY: I'm not doing anything, it's you who's actively... you're getting verbs and adjectives confused here. There's a difference between...

HUGO: Being annoying and being annoying.

HARTLEY: Yes. Yes.

HUGO: So which one am I?

HARTLEY: A bit of both, to be honest. And you're making it worse.

HUGO: By asking about daddy?

HARTLEY: By asking pointless questions. The money is out there. Somewhere. You think daddy would have left us with nothing? Is that what you're saying?

HUGO: No, he's left us a fortune.

HUGO gently kicks the box at his feet.

HUGO: At the moment it's all tied up in household goods...

HARTLEY: You're about to make me fucking angry.

HUGO gasps.

HUGO: Hartley...

HARTLEY: Where's all this come from anyway?

HUGO: All what?

HARTLEY: All this money money pirate chest nonsense.

HUGO: I've been reading.

HARTLEY: It's none of your concern. Reading what?

HUGO shrugs.

HUGO: The stuff.

HARTLEY: The stuff? Oh good. That's what I like, a bit of clarity.

HUGO: Where do you see it coming from then? The money.

HARTLEY: If you ask that question again – Are you a solicitor?

HUGO: Pardon?

HARTLEY: Are you a solicitor?

HUGO: I don't understand.

HARTLEY: It's not a trick. Are you a solicitor?

HUGO: I...I don't know.

HARTLEY: Yes you do. Answer me.

HUGO: You know the answer.

HARTLEY: Stop playing games and answer the bloody question. Are you a –

HUGO stamps his foot hard on the floor.

He looks at the point on the floor where he just stamped for a moment.

HUGO: Mouse.

Beat.

HARTLEY: Let's check the bedroom.

HUGO: You mean that room with a bed in it?

HARTLEY: Yes, the bedroom.

HUGO: Hang on, don't want to tread...

HUGO scrapes the remains of the mouse off the sole of his shoe on a ledge by the window.

HUGO: Busy out there, isn't it?

HARTLEY: Too bloody busy.

HUGO: Lots going on I imagine. Out there. Lots to do.

HUGO: Not for us there isn't.

Beat.

HUGO: Lots of different...you know...

HARTLEY: No I don't know Hugo. Lots of different what? Ways to get run over? Diseases to catch?

HUGO: Jobs and stuff.

HARTLEY: Jobs?

HUGO: And stuff.

HARTLEY: Why on earth would you bring that up?

HUGO: Just making an observation.

HARTLEY: Jobs?

HUGO: Yeah, like...you know, jobs.

HARTLEY: What the hell's that got to do with –

HUGO: Nothing.

HARTLEY: – Anything?

HUGO: Nothing. Forget it.

HARTLEY stares at HUGO as he turns and picks something up.

HUGO: Sell that. Definitely...

HARTLEY: Why did you say that?

HUGO: Say what?

HARTLEY: About there being jobs down here.

HUGO: I was just making an observation.

HARTLEY: Why though?

HUGO: Because there are.

HARTLEY: We have jobs.

HUGO: Right.

HARTLEY: Don't we?

HUGO: Yes.

HARTLEY: So why did you say it?

HUGO: I just meant if all this stuff didn't quite keep us...till the money...

HARTLEY keeps staring.

HUGO: And then just in case, in the slim, very slim chance that the inheritance didn't...that it wasn't...then we'd already have...you know, money. From the, from the jobs...that we would have...

Beat.

HARTLEY: Okay then.

HUGO: Okay?

HARTLEY: Yes, let's get jobs. Here. In London.

HUGO: Really?

HARTLEY: Yep. Let's get ourselves a pair of London jobs.

HUGO: Right, okay. Good.

HARTLEY: Good. How, exactly?

HUGO: Pardon?

HARTLEY: How do you go about getting a job in London, Hugo?

HUGO: Well...

Pause.

HARTLEY: Go on.

HUGO: We'd have to ask. I don't think they're just giving them away.

HARTLEY: And who do we ask?

HUGO: Well...

HUGO clears his throat.

HARTLEY: Come on. It's tomorrow morning. You're going off to get a job. You step out onto the street. Onto the road, out there. What do you do?

Beat.

HARTLEY: Who do you ask?

Beat.

HARTLEY: Where do you turn?

Beat.

HARTLEY: I asked you a question.

HUGO: I don't know. I don't know.

HARTLEY: You don't know.

HUGO: I don't know.

HARTLEY: Maybe you could go out in your costume. In your little fluffy costume.

HUGO: Hartley...

HARTLEY: Have I made my point?

HUGO: Why do you have to do that?

HARTLEY: Do what?

HUGO: Be mean.

HARTLEY: Because otherwise it doesn't go in, does it?

He pushes his fist into HUGO's temple. HUGO backs away.

HUGO: Doesn't mean you have to be such a...

HARTLEY: Ten minutes.

HUGO: Ten minutes...

HARTLEY: Ten.

HUGO: 'Oooh, ten minutes! Ten minutes!'

HARTLEY: It's the principle.

Pause. HUGO takes out an invitation.

HUGO: So are we going to this then?

HARTLEY turns, sees the invitation.

HARTLEY: Put that away. Put it away.

HUGO: We could go for a bit maybe.

HARTLEY: No, absolutely not.

HUGO: Why?

HARTLEY: Because I said so.

HUGO: Maybe just for a few minutes. Someone might know daddy.

HARTLEY: Don't be ridiculous. We're not going to a party. Put it away.

HUGO puts the invitation in his pocket.

HARTLEY: There's a train leaving at seven. We take anything of value, burn the rest and get the bloody hell back to civilisation.

HUGO: We could meet his associates. Ask them about –

HARTLEY: No one will see us down here. No one will ever know. Do you understand?

HUGO: Where are we going to live?

HARTLEY: Back home.

HUGO: We don't have a home though, do we? He sold it. Before he –

HARTLEY: So you'd rather stay down here? Hmm?

HARTLEY sweeps his arm across the room.

HARTLEY: Here?

HUGO: No, but there could be someone there –

HARTLEY: What's that?

HUGO: What, where?

HARTLEY: There behind you.

HUGO turns, picks up a bag of hair.

HUGO: It's a bag of human hair.

HARTLEY: Urgh. Sell it.

HUGO drops it into the box.

HUGO: Hartley.

HARTLEY: Yes Huggy Bear?

HUGO: Don't call me that.

HARTLEY: I thought you liked it. Huggy.

HUGO: I said don't! Or I'll call you –

HARTLEY: Okay, okay. What's wrong?

HUGO: Why do you think he did it?

Beat. HARTLEY rubs his eyes, then moves over and holds HUGO.
He kisses his forehead.

There is a knock at the door. They both spin to face it.

HARTLEY: What was that?

HUGO: The door.

HARTLEY: Why did it make a noise?

HUGO: Because someone wants to come in through it.

HARTLEY: Don't open it.

HUGO: I think someone wants to come in though.

Another knock. HUGO moves over and looks through the peep hole.

HUGO: It's a man.

HARTLEY: Are you sure? It could be a woman with short hair.

HUGO looks again.

HUGO: No I think it's a man.

HARTLEY: Shit. How do I look?

HUGO: Kind of...forlorn.

HARTLEY: How's my hair?

HUGO: Greasy.

HARTLEY: Too greasy or not greasy enough?

HUGO: Well, greasy. So...

HARTLEY: And that's bad?

HUGO: Yes.

HARTLEY: So what's good, dry hair?

HUGO: Not dry, no.

HARTLEY: So what then, moist? Damp?

HUGO: Glossy.

HARTLEY: I thought you said mine was glossy.

HUGO: No yours is greasy.

HARTLEY: Dammit. Give me the hair dryer.

Another knock.

HUGO: I should probably open it.

HARTLEY: Don't open it!

HARTLEY breathes into his hands. Sniffs.

HARTLEY: Do you have a breath mint?

HUGO: Why?

HARTLEY: My breath smells.

HUGO: That's your hands.

HARTLEY smells his hands.

HARTLEY: Urgh. Why do my hands smell?

HUGO: I don't know.

HARTLEY: Have they always smelt like this?

HUGO: I don't know.

HARTLEY: It's like curdled milk.

HUGO: I know. I'm opening the door now.

HARTLEY: No! I won't meet her with greasy hair and smelly hands. She'll think I'm an animal.

HUGO: I'm fairly certain it's a man.

HARTLEY: I'm going for a quick bath. Keep her there.

A gruff male voice from the other side of the door.

VOICE: *(O.S.)* Open the fuckin...come on! Open this fucking door!

HARTLEY and HUGO drop to the floor.

HARTLEY: I don't think she's my type.

Long pause.

HUGO slowly goes over and checks the peephole.

HUGO: He's gone.

HARTLEY: Thank God for that. What do you think he wanted?

HUGO: I don't know.

HARTLEY: Right, we have to act quickly. Anything with the crest on it. Anything with daddy's name, or face or... anything, just...

HARTLEY starts frantically looking around the flat for evidence of his father.

HUGO does the same. They continue as they talk. Occasionally HARTLEY drops something into the sell box.

HARTLEY: I hate this place. So loud. Everyone's so angry. And violent.

HUGO: Violent?

HARTLEY: They carry knives you know.

HUGO: Who do?

HARTLEY: Londoners. They carry knives around with them.

HUGO: What for?

HARTLEY: What do you think? In case they get into an argument and their vocabulary fails them.

HUGO: I wouldn't worry. You're an expert on knives.

HARTLEY: There's not much to know. One end's blunt, the other end's sharp. As long as you keep the sharp end pointing away from you you're in a pretty strong position.

HUGO: Do you think that man had a knife?

HARTLEY: I don't know.

HUGO stops searching.

HUGO: You don't think daddy was having an affair do you?

HARTLEY: I'm sorry?

HUGO: Coming down here all the time. And then doing what he did. I just thought it might be because he was having an affair.

HARTLEY: Have you been watching television again?

HUGO: No. I was just thinking out loud.

HARTLEY: Well don't think out loud, think in your head. And don't think things like that. Think about something else.

HUGO: Like what?

HARTLEY: I don't know, goats. Recite the periodic table, do some long division. I don't care.

HUGO: I've been thinking about mother.

HARTLEY: Don't think about mother!

HUGO: Why not?

HARTLEY: Because if you think about mother then you'll think about what happened, and if you think about what happened you'll start conjuring up all sorts of stupid reasons for it.

HUGO: There must've been a reason though. Otherwise it wouldn't have happened.

HARTLEY: Whatever it was, I'm sure it was logical, considered, and had our best interests at heart.

HUGO looks around the room.

HUGO: Right. Best interests.

HARTLEY: Father loved us very much and he wouldn't have left us in a situation we can't handle. Do you understand that?

HUGO: Yep. Yeah...

Beat.

HUGO: Except, some of the things he did. When he was alive. They weren't very nice things to do. To your own sons. Really.

HARTLEY: He loved us very much.

HUGO: And even what he did, to mother and...I can't figure out, you know, why...why he...

HARTLEY takes the tie from his pocket and shoves it into HUGO's face.

HARTLEY: Look at that. Look at it. Remember who you are. Just remember who you're talking about.

Beat. HARTLEY relents.

HUGO: I'm allowed to ask why.

HARTLEY: And I'm allowed to tell you I don't know yet.

A key in the door. It's opened.

HUGO and HARTLEY scramble into the corners, crouching.

TEDDY enters, drunk.

TEDDY: Who's in here? Where are you?

He spots HARTLEY crouched in the corner facing the wall.

TEDDY: What are you doing in here?

Beat.

TEDDY: Oi, I'm talking to you!

HARTLEY stands up, blinking.

HARTLEY: Goodness, I appear to have wandered into the wrong pub basement and crouched in the corner.

HUGO gets to his feet.

HUGO: Strange, I appear to have done the exact same thing.

HARTLEY: Well, we'll get out of your hair.

They make to leave. TEDDY stops them with a hand on HARTLEY's chest.

TEDDY: What the fuck are you doing in here?

HARTLEY: There's been a mistake. Please. My brother is ill. Aren't you Hugo?

HUGO coughs.

HARTLEY: He may have the palsy. We don't know.

TEDDY: Where is he?

HARTLEY: Please, I have a weak heart and no valuables on my person.

TEDDY: I asked you a question. Where is he?

HUGO: Who?

TEDDY: The old man.

HARTLEY: The...

TEDDY: The old man! Where is he? You know who I'm talking about. What've you done to him?

HUGO: You knew him?

TEDDY: Course I fucking knew him. Now where is he? If you've touched a single hair on his chin –

HARTLEY: No, he's...how did you know him?

TEDDY: Who are you?

TEDDY looks at HUGO's face for a moment.

TEDDY: Who the fuck are you?

HARTLEY: I was about to ask you the same question, except without the profanity which I found a bit rude to be honest.

HUGO: We're his sons.

HARTLEY: Shut up Hugo.

TEDDY: Beg pardon?

HUGO: We're his sons.

HARTLEY: Hugo for christ's sake!

TEDDY: His what?

He grabs HARTLEY.

TEDDY: His what!

HARTLEY: Children. Sons. He was our father, we were his sons. It was a mutual arrangement we had.

TEDDY lets go of HARTLEY.

TEDDY: Children?

HARTLEY: And who are you?

TEDDY: You're his sons..?

HARTLEY: Excuse me, I asked –

TEDDY: Where is he?

HUGO: He's dead. Our father's dead.

TEDDY: Dead?

HARTLEY: Yes dead.

TEDDY: Is it serious?

HARTLEY: Quite serious, yes. He's dead.

TEDDY: No...

Pause.

TEDDY sits down.

TEDDY: I can't believe it. I cannot believe it.

HARTLEY: Yes, we're having a bit of a shocker ourselves.

TEDDY: Kids...how many? Did he have? How many?

HUGO: Just us. We're twins.

TEDDY: Twins? Fuck me.

TEDDY looks up at them.

TEDDY: Are you identical?

HUGO and HARTLEY share a look.

HARTLEY: No.

HUGO: Are you okay? You seem to be in shock.

TEDDY: No one told me.

HUGO: Well it happened very recently.

TEDDY: I can't believe it.

HARTLEY: We don't really have any contact with his London associates.

TEDDY: He never told me that.

HARTLEY: Well he probably wouldn't have told you himself...

TEDDY: Two boys. This whole time he had two boys.

HARTLEY: He...what?

TEDDY: He never mentioned you. Never said he had kids.

HARTLEY swallows.

HUGO: Did you know him well?

TEDDY: I looked after him when he was down here.

HUGO: Looked after him?

TEDDY: You know that pub up there? It's mine.

Beat.

TEDDY: I looked after him. All this time...

TEDDY shakes his head.

HUGO: Are you okay?

TEDDY: Yeah no no yeah. Yeah no...yeah.

Beat.

HARTLEY: Which one?

TEDDY: I'm fine. I'm fine. I just need a minute.

HUGO looks to HARTLEY, who silently and surreptitiously continues his search.

He moves over to a picture in a frame. He tries to take out the picture. It slips from his grasp and clatters onto the floor.

HARTLEY: Sorry. That was probably about a minute anyway. Would you say, roughly?

TEDDY: Where's his body?

HARTLEY: Listen, sir, we're in rather a hurry. If you could give us half an hour to clear our things up, we could be –

TEDDY: What have you done with his body?

HUGO: He was cremated.

TEDDY: He wanted to be buried. He always said he wanted to be buried.

HARTLEY: I don't know what to say.

TEDDY: He wanted to be buried. I was holding onto things. For inside his coffin.

HARTLEY: He must've changed his mind.

TEDDY: I made him a promise. We had a promise.

HARTLEY: I'm telling you he changed his mind.

TEDDY: How do you know?

HARTLEY: Because I was the one scraping his head off the walls.

TEDDY: You what?

HARTLEY: Shotgun in the mouth. He did mother first.

TEDDY: Fuck.

HARTLEY: That's what I said.

TEDDY: Suicide?

HUGO: Yeah.

TEDDY: When was the funeral?

HUGO: What funeral?

TEDDY: I thought you said he was cremated.

HUGO: He was.

TEDDY: I can't believe he did that.

HARTLEY: I know.

TEDDY: I just can't fathom it.

HARTLEY: I know.

TEDDY: What a cunt.

HARTLEY: I – pardon?

TEDDY: The bastard owed me money.

HARTLEY: Did he?

TEDDY: That's why I'm here. Collection day. We agreed.

HARTLEY: Okay, well sir, let's get you paid and you can go
     back to...wherever you came from. Hugo, what cash do
     you have on you?

HUGO: Really?

HARTLEY: What do you have on you?

HUGO: But we need –

HARTLEY: I won't ask again.

     HUGO takes out his coin bag and looks through it.

HARTLEY: How much did he owe you?

TEDDY: The exact amount was a point of debate. But roughly...quarter of a mil.

Beat.

HUGO puts his coin bag away.

HARTLEY: A quarter of a mill...ion?

TEDDY: Give or take.

HUGO: As in two hundred and fifty thousand?

TEDDY: As I said it was a point of debate.

HARTLEY: And when you say point of debate...

TEDDY: I reckon it's nearer three hundred.

HARTLEY: That's a shame.

HUGO surveys the basement.

HUGO: I can't help but feel he was overcharged.

TEDDY: I told you I looked after him.

HARTLEY: You looked after him? With what? What cost a quarter of a million pounds?

TEDDY: Something that money can't buy.

HARTLEY: If money can't buy it how can he possibly owe you?

TEDDY: Fuck it!

TEDDY slams his foot into a box. Composes himself.

TEDDY: So you're gonna tell me you ain't got it now.

HARTLEY: I'm afraid so.

TEDDY: Not easy moving that much money in a hurry.

HARTLEY: Exactly.

TEDDY: You'll need time to come to terms with it all. Am I right?

HARTLEY: Yep. Yes that's right.

TEDDY: You need some time. I understand that.

HARTLEY: Thank you for being so reasonable. Well, you probably have lots to be getting on with –

TEDDY: No, I understand how it is. So tomorrow morning then.

HARTLEY: Hah?

TEDDY: For the money. I'll come round tomorrow. Sometime before lunch.

HARTLEY: We're leaving in a couple of hours.

TEDDY: No you're not.

HARTLEY: Yes we are.

TEDDY: No you're not.

HARTLEY: We have a train to catch at seven.

TEDDY: What's the rush? There's a bed through there. No charge.

HARTLEY: Nope, no I'm afraid that's –

TEDDY: Don't worry about trains. There's loads of them.

HARTLEY: When we said we didn't have the money. We don't actually have the money.

HUGO: We have no money.

HARTLEY: As in zero pounds.

TEDDY: What are you talking about? He was a rich cunt.

HUGO: Everything's gone. The estate.

HARTLEY: The art collection. Stocks.

HUGO: He sold it all.

TEDDY: When?

HARTLEY: Right before he...

TEDDY: What, without telling you?

HARTLEY: We were...unaware, until –

TEDDY: You're having a laugh, ain't you?

HARTLEY: I wish we were. It's...it's all gone.

HUGO: There's nothing left.

TEDDY: No, this is bullshit.

HARTLEY: I assure you it's not.

TEDDY: This is fucking horse shit.

HARTLEY: It really isn't any kind of faeces. Please, I'm just a humble butcher. My brother is a goatherd.

TEDDY: A goatherd?

HARTLEY: He herds goats. We've just lost our parents. We have no money and no means of getting any. We've never even been to London before.

HUGO: I thought it was an island.

HARTLEY: He did.

Beat.

HARTLEY: We're hoping to hire a solicitor.

TEDDY: I'm not interested in fucking solicitors. I don't deal with solicitors. I came here to collect what I'm owed, and you two ain't leaving until I get it, is that clear?

HUGO: Please, mister. This can all be straightened out in good time.

TEDDY: He's done this on purpose, I know he has.

HARTLEY: There's really nothing we can do for you right now.

TEDDY stares at HUGO.

TEDDY: You look just like him.

HUGO: So I've been told.

Pause. He stares.

TEDDY: So your father's offed himself, and your mum.

HUGO: Yes.

TEDDY: He's left you with no money, nowhere to live and nothing to do...And he's forced you out of your comfort zone and down to the big, dirty old city for the first time in your lives.

HARTLEY: That's more or less how things stand.

TEDDY: He's sent you down here looking like a pair of referees from a croquet match. He's delivered you here...to me.

HARTLEY: I don't think that's quite –

TEDDY: And now you feel lost and alone.

HUGO: Yes.

TEDDY: And very scared I imagine.

HUGO: And hungry as well.

Beat. TEDDY grins.

TEDDY: Now I understand. Yeah, I get it now.

HARTLEY: Good. Well at least that's sorted. If you could give us a few more minutes, we won't be long...

TEDDY: He was a smart man, your father.

HARTLEY: Yes, Oxford educated. And if you'd keep all this to yourself we'd be very grateful...

TEDDY: I provided him with things money can't buy. And now he's left me the most priceless gift of all. His most precious possessions.

TEDDY moves over to HUGO and starts stroking his face.

TEDDY: Oh, you are precious.

HUGO: Hartley?

HARTLEY: Don't make any sudden movements old boy. Just stand still and let him stroke your face.

SCENE TWO

TEDDY has fixed himself a glass of water. He drops in an Alka-Seltzer tablet. The three of them watch the water fizz.

TEDDY: See, I never had any sons. Proteges, sure. Loads of them. I had proteges coming out of my fucking arse. But an actual son, my own flesh and blood...you need to pass on your bloodline, don't you? Your genes, you want them to carry on. I want a young me, someone to inherit my strength of character. My instinct for war. The overactive mucus gland will probably get thrown in there as well, but you know, rough with the smooth.

He takes a swig of the fizzy water.

TEDDY: I wanna be a teacher, you know? I wanna be a teacher.

He is still looking at HUGO.

TEDDY: Your dad's genes. They must've been like the fucking Persian army. Going in there, dominating everything. 'Right, you're gonna look just like us and there's fuck all you can do about it.'

HARTLEY: He was more of a mummy's boy.

TEDDY: Oh yeah?

HUGO: She was a beautiful woman.

HARTLEY: He means on the inside. Physically she was a hog.

HUGO: Hmmn.

TEDDY: Ugly was she?

HUGO: She had a beautiful spirit.

HARTLEY: You wouldn't have guessed from the outside. She looked like a spaniel.

TEDDY: Makes sense, that. All things considered.

HUGO: How do you mean?

TEDDY: Well, you don't borrow your mate's Ferrari if you've got a Porsche at home in the garage, do you?

Beat.

HARTLEY: Daddy drove a Volvo.

TEDDY: Exactly.

HARTLEY: What?

TEDDY: I'm just saying he came to me for my services. And we wouldn't have done that if he was getting serviced at home.

HARTLEY: He did though. There was an engineer in the village used to do it for free.

TEDDY: Forget the car thing. It's a euphemism.

HARTLEY: A euphemism for what?

TEDDY: What do you usually use euphemisms for?

Beat.

TEDDY: The kind of thing you're not allowed to discuss at the dinner table.

HARTLEY: Oh...immigration.

TEDDY: No...

HUGO: The time daddy shot that man in the knee and had to pay his daughter's university fees.

TEDDY: What? No. Forget it. The point is I provided a service to which your dad was a willing patron.

HUGO: What service?

TEDDY: I have my fingers in many pies. Apart from the pie trade, that's a fortress. But mainly I look after people. I look after my boys and girls. You're incredibly lucky I was an associate of your father's. Some people in my position would exploit you. Abuse you even. But I treat my boys and girls well. You'll have a place to live. Nice clothes. Food to eat. Maybe even friends.

HARTLEY: We have a friend already, thank you.

TEDDY: A friend?

HARTLEY: Yes.

TEDDY: You have one friend?

HARTLEY: Well how...how many friends can one expect to have?

TEDDY: More than one darlin'.

HARTLEY: We're perfectly happy with our social circle.

TEDDY: Circle? How's it a circle with one friend?

HARTLEY: We have a friend and we're happy with that arrangement, thank you.

HUGO: Who is it?

HARTLEY: Who is what?

HUGO: Who's our friend?

HARTLEY: Friendly Tom.

HUGO: Friendly Tom is 88 and blind.

HARTLEY: So?

HUGO: He thinks you're the ghost of his unit commander from the Great War.

HARTLEY: He's a mate.

HUGO: He doesn't even like you that much.

HARTLEY: Who says?

HUGO: He does. Said you're a bit clingy.

HARTLEY: Clingy?

HUGO: He has a life outside us you know. The veteran's association, the allotment. He's in demand.

HARTLEY: You're telling me this now?

HUGO: You weren't getting the hints.

HARTLEY: Well screw him. He can mush his own supper from now on.

Beat.

HARTLEY: Don't tell him I said that.

TEDDY: Forget friendly Tom, the blind old cunt. You're gonna make more friends than you know what to do with. They're gonna drink you up.

HUGO: 88-year-old friends, or normal ones?

TEDDY's phone starts ringing.

TEDDY: Oh, hang on.

He answers it.

TEDDY: Clarence...can...can I call you back? I'm a bit busy sweetheart. Downstairs, yeah, yeah. Listen, we all set for tonight? Excellent. I've got a surprise...you're not gonna believe those eyes of yours. Tell Roderigo he won't be needed tonight after all. Stick him in the hostel, he's always popular. Lovely...you what? Well don't pick at it...no, don't pick at it. You'll make it worse. Have you still got that cream? I'll take a look at it. I said I would, just don't touch it. Right.

He hangs up.

TEDDY: What was I saying?

HARTLEY: You were telling Clarence not to pick at it.

TEDDY: I mean before the phone call.

HUGO: Friends.

TEDDY: Friends, that's right. You two ever had any...special friends?

HARTLEY: I really think we're underselling Friendly Tom. He's a pretty special guy.

TEDDY: No, I mean special friends.

HUGO: You mean girls?

TEDDY: Or boys. We're all God's children in the dark.

HARTLEY: No, we've never had any 'special' friends, thank you very much. And you really have no right to ask that kind of question.

TEDDY: Let me tell you a story about your daddy. You wanna hear a story? About your daddy? Here's a good one. On this one occasion, he'd asked to spend some quality private time with a special friend. Young man called Benny. Lovely boy, Benny. Nothing unusual about that. Anyway, they were together in the bedroom for about two hours, and when it came time for him to leave, he wouldn't come out. He'd jammed the door shut and plugged the lock.

HARTLEY: This is ridiculous. Hugo let's check the bedroom.

HUGO: I'll come through in a minute.

HARTLEY: Hugo, the bedroom.

HUGO: In a minute.

HARTLEY: No, now.

HUGO: I want to hear the rest of the story.

HARTLEY: It's nonsense. It's all made up.

HUGO: Like a pirate story.

Beat.

TEDDY: I'll continue then shall I? So, err...right. So the door was jammed shut and we couldn't hear a peep from the inside. So we huffed and we puffed and we banged and shouted and cursed. Nothing. Not a peep. Eventually we kicked the door in. First thing to hit us was the fumes.

A big waft of chemicals, like walking into a science lab. Honestly, our eyes were streaming. And your dad, get this, your dad was sat bollock naked on the edge of the bed with this weird little grin on his face. And poor Benny was lying comatose on the floor. And I mean literally in a coma. And your daddy had shaved him completely bald. He'd sheared him all over. Every single hair on his body gone.

HUGO moves to the sell box and takes out the bag of human hair.

TEDDY: How funny is that! He must've brought his own shaver and everything. I mean, we're permissive, but Christ...

HUGO: That's awful.

TEDDY laughs.

TEDDY: I forgave him though. I always forgave him.

HARTLEY: Don't listen to a word of it Hugo.

HUGO: That's...did he really do that?

TEDDY: You should've seen him when he got his wind. Hours and hours on end he could go for.

HARTLEY: Hugo, I'm telling you it's all nonsense.

HUGO: How would you know?

Beat.

HARTLEY: Beg your pardon?

HUGO: How would you know anything about daddy? I don't.

HARTLEY: He was our father.

HUGO: So?

HARTLEY: What do you mean so? He was our father.

HUGO: What does that prove?

HARTLEY: What the hell's gotten into you?

HUGO: I'm just curious.

HARTLEY: Curious?

HUGO: Look at this place. Aren't you a bit curious? Why was he down here?

Beat.

HUGO: He lived here Hartley. All that time away from us, this is where he actually lived. Is this what you pictured? Is this where you saw him staying?

TEDDY: He's his father's son. You've got his fire in you. I can feel it.

HARTLEY: We told you, he was a mummy's boy.

TEDDY: No, not this one. He's got his daddy inside him, running through his blood.

HARTLEY: That's a load of shit. Daddy didn't even –

HUGO: What? Daddy didn't even what? Go on, say it.

HARTLEY: Nothing.

HUGO: Say it.

HARTLEY: I don't know what I was going to say.

HUGO: Daddy didn't even like me. That's what you were about to say, wasn't it? He didn't really care for me. You on the other hand –

HARTLEY: Oh for God's sake-

HUGO: By his side on shoots. Laughing at his jokes about the gays. Polishing his rifle. Polishing his trophies. Polishing his ornamental crockery. You just loved to polish.

HARTLEY: I had the knack for it. You always left it streaky.

HUGO: I don't care.

HARTLEY: You have to buff in a circular motion.

HUGO: I said I don't care. Why should I care? He made his choice.

HARTLEY: Don't be silly. It wasn't that simple.

HUGO: You think we knew him? We never knew him.

HARTLEY points to TEDDY.

HARTLEY: What about him? Who's he? You walk in here, claiming to know our father. You could be anyone, you could be one of those degenerates who sit on the floor outside.

HUGO: Daddy owed him money.

HARTLEY: And you're just going to trust him? You're just going to believe everything he says?

TEDDY fondles his tie, it has the family crest on it.

HUGO: What choice do we have?

Beat.

HUGO: Look around you, Hartley. I'm asking, what choice –

HARTLEY abruptly bursts into song.

HARTLEY: In the fair fields of wheat and heather fa la la la la la la la la!

HUGO: No –

HARTLEY: Let the children wander free forever fa la la la la la la la la!

HUGO: Not now –

HARTLEY: Keep them plump and well on meat and dairy fa la la la la la la la la!

HUGO: Hartley please –

HARTLEY: And forever more may they be merry fala la la la la la la la!

Beat. HARTLEY and HUGO look at each other.

HARTLEY: Two three four...

Now HUGO and HARTLEY sing in unison.

HARTLEY & HUGO: May the song of nature be always in our hearts! And may our sacks be fat with grain before the winter starts! And may the sound of birdsong hang so sweetly in the sky! And may the rain keep wet what's wet, and the sun keep dry what's dry!

HARTLEY nods to HUGO. HUGO sighs.

HUGO: And so we kneel before our saviour watching from the sky.

TEDDY: Beautiful. That was beautiful.

HARTLEY: We're leaving London. Now.

HUGO: We have nowhere to go.

HARTLEY: Yes we do. Somewhere that's not here.

HUGO: Where though? Where? Hartley I'm asking where –

HARTLEY: Shut up! I hate this fucking place. I hate the buildings, I hate the people, and I hate what it's doing to you.

HUGO: I've been here three hours.

HARTLEY: You're coming with me.

HUGO: No I'm not.

HARTLEY: I won't have you staying here with him.

HUGO: In case I turn into daddy?

HARTLEY slaps HUGO across the face.

They stare at each other.

HUGO: Ow.

TEDDY: Boys. There's no need for violence. Let's have a drink, calm down a bit. I make my own gin you know. You're not allergic to penicillin are you?

HARTLEY: We don't belong here.

HUGO: We don't belong anywhere.

HARTLEY: Collect your things. We're going to the station.

HUGO: Okay...

HARTLEY: Good get your things.

HUGO: Okay, so you get off the train at the other end. You're on the train platform. What do you do? Who do you ask? Where do you turn?

HARTLEY: Don't get smart with me.

HUGO: I'm asking though. I'm actually asking.

HARTLEY: And what's our other option then? Hah? What's your solution?

HUGO takes out the party invitation. TEDDY notices it.

HARTLEY makes to grab for it but TEDDY gets there first.

TEDDY: Hello. Ha ha! Where'd you get this?

HUGO: It was on his person. When we found him.

TEDDY: Unbelievable. This is what brought you down? That is funny. It's just upstairs you know. Tonight. Just a few old friends. Nothing big. But if you fancy it...

HARTLEY: No. Definitely not.

TEDDY: They're quite famous around certain circles, my parties. He was a regular.

TEDDY gestures to the invitation.

TEDDY: You'll appreciate the kind of clientele we get in. Your kinds of people.

HARTLEY: We said no thank you.

TEDDY: We had a member of the royal family in last week. Lee, his name was.

Beat.

TEDDY: Yeah, Lee. He was a minor royal. You'll be guests of honour. I know they'd love to meet you after hearing such tragic news.

HARTLEY: The answer's no. No parties. No shindigs. No hootenanies or box socials. Nothing and no one. Just home.

TEDDY: He's a grumpy sod isn't he? How about you? Fancy it? Meeting some of your daddy's friends? Some nice food?

HARTLEY: Hugo.

HUGO: Okay.

HARTLEY: Good. What?

HUGO: A party sounds nice.

HARTLEY: Don't you dare disobey me.

TEDDY: You do whatever you want.

HARTLEY: Ten minutes. Remember. Daddy's gone now, so –

TEDDY: It's your decision son.

HARTLEY: It's not your decision, it's our decision.

TEDDY: I promise to tell you more about your daddy.

HARTLEY: You won't be able to wear your costume. Huggy Bear.

TEDDY: Everything you wanna know. Anything at all. I've got a lot of stories.

HARTLEY: Don't make this mistake.

TEDDY: A party's never a mistake.

HARTLEY: We've both made mistakes in the past, but I'm telling you, do not make this mistake.

TEDDY: You need to lighten up a bit son. What was the last party you went to?

HUGO & HARTLEY: Aunt Bridget and Uncle Cecil's thirty-fifth wedding anniversary.

TEDDY: I see. Any good?

HUGO: We don't like to talk about it.

HARTLEY: Objects were thrown. Brains were damaged.

TEDDY: Well it sounds like you're ready to be shown a good time. I'm telling you it's what your father would've wanted.

HARTLEY: And how the hell would you know what he would've wanted?

TEDDY laughs.

TEDDY: If there's one thing I fucking know, it's what that old man wanted. Believe me.

HARTLEY: Do you believe him?

HUGO: How could I possibly know any different?

HARTLEY: This is a man's legacy you're playing with.

HUGO: Legacy?

HARTLEY: If people know about this –

HUGO: Know about what?

HARTLEY: If anyone finds out. We'll be destroyed.

HUGO: He didn't really give us much choice though, did he?

HARTLEY: What are you talking about?

HUGO: We're stuck here. We're stranded.

HARTLEY: And you think going to a party's the answer?

HUGO: I don't know what the answer is. But we have to start somewhere.

HARTLEY: Just remember. Remember what happens when you're left on your own.

TEDDY: He won't be on his own. He'll be with me. And his new friends.

HARTLEY: Ten minutes. Ten minutes Hugo...

HUGO: What did you learn in ten minutes? What did you learn in those ten minutes before I was born? Hah? What did I miss out on?

HARTLEY: It's the principle.

TEDDY: Does he make all your decisions for you? Or do you ever get to think for yourself?

HUGO: Why don't you come too? You should come Hartley.

TEDDY: More the merrier.

HUGO: Come with us. We could ask about him.

HARTLEY: Do you understand what you're doing Hugo? You're ruining us. You're ruining the family.

HUGO: What family?

HARTLEY: How are we supposed to rebuild? If people know about this then how the hell are we supposed to salvage what we have?

HUGO: What is there to salvage?

HARTLEY: The crest. The family crest.

TEDDY: You mean that? With the lions...?

TEDDY fondles his tie with the family crest on. HARTLEY notices.

TEDDY: Do you like it? Present. From the patriarch of your family dynasty.

HARTLEY lunges at TEDDY, pulling at his tie. TEDDY throws him away with vicious efficiency and pins his face against the wall.

TEDDY: It belongs to me. It's mine.

He lets HARTLEY go.

HARTLEY: Enjoy yourselves.

HUGO: Where are you going?

HARTLEY: You think I'm going to stay here? Wait for you?

HUGO: Are you leaving?

HARTLEY: Sit in this shitty little dank basement, listening to our family being destroyed upstairs? That's what you expect me to do?

HUGO: You're leaving me?

HARTLEY: No, you're leaving me.

He exits.

TEDDY: Ah well, we'll have fun anyway.

Beat. HUGO stares at the door.

TEDDY: Won't we? Eh?

HUGO: Love Heart.

Beat.

TEDDY: Listen, time's ticking. We need to sort you out a costume.

HUGO: Costume?

TEDDY: Oh yeah. You'll need a party frock. I told you, you'll be the belle of the ball.

TEDDY moves over and starts rubbing his flank.

HUGO: I should go after him.

TEDDY: Don't you worry about him.

HUGO: I'm not very good on my own.

TEDDY: Come on, let's get you looking all nice for your new friends.

TEDDY hums the hymn from earlier. A nasty laugh.

TEDDY: Here, let me tell you a story about your daddy...

SCENE THREE

Night. HARTLEY sits alone. He picks up a book from a pile by the sofa and flicks through it. A piece of prescription paper falls from between the pages onto the floor. He picks it up and examines it.

After a moment, HUGO enters. He is wearing white pumps, small denim shorts, a vest and a denim jacket. He shuffles into the room, head bowed, and sits next to HARTLEY.

HARTLEY: How was it?

Pause. HUGO breathes deeply.

HARTLEY: Are you okay?

Beat.

HARTLEY: What's wrong?

Beat.

HARTLEY: Say something.

HUGO: I didn't enjoy myself.

HARTLEY: What happened? Was it like aunt Bridget and Uncle Cecil's thirty-fifth wedding anniversary?

HUGO: Not exactly.

HARTLEY: Hugo what's wrong?

HUGO: I was made to...

HARTLEY: What? Made to what?

HUGO: Do things.

HARTLEY: What things?

Beat.

HUGO: Do you remember that time when the caretaker invited us into his den?

HARTLEY: Yes.

HUGO: Do you remember the video he showed us, of the two men...

HARTLEY: Yes.

HUGO: Well there was some of that.

Beat.

HUGO: And do you remember what Father Kilcannon was caught doing to Charlie Spencer in the vestry after choir practice?

HARTLEY: Yes.

HUGO: Well there was quite a lot of that.

Beat.

HUGO: And do you remember when the Charterhouse boys used to climb over the fence and chase me?

HARTLEY: Yes.

HUGO: And I'd cry out for daddy as loud as I could, and I'd keep screaming, and at the very last minute daddy would appear out of the darkness and save me?

HARTLEY: Yes I remember.

HUGO: There was none of that.

HUGO fights back tears. They hold hands.

HARTLEY: Are you hungry?

HUGO: No.

Beat.

HUGO: They were chanting. They were all chanting our name.

Beat.

HUGO: Where did you go?

HARTLEY: For a walk.

HUGO: How was it?

HARTLEY: Strange. Very strange.

Beat.

HARTLEY: There were people everywhere, but I didn't know who they were. They were all walking, but I didn't know where they were going. They were speaking to each other, but I couldn't understand what they were saying. I couldn't work out what any of the buildings were for, and the maze of roads made me dizzy.

And there were noises all the time. Loud noises that I couldn't decipher.

Beat.

HARTLEY: And everyone was staring. They were all staring at me.

HUGO: Why?

HARTLEY: I have no idea.

HUGO: Were they angry?

HARTLEY: Not angry, no. Terrified. They were all absolutely terrified.

Beat. HUGO sings very quietly.

HUGO: May the song of nature be always in our hearts... And may our sacks be fat with grain before the winter starts... And may the sound of birdsong hang so sweetly in the sky... And may the rain keep wet what's wet, and... and...

HARTLEY: The sun keep dry what's dry.

Pause.

HUGO: Do you ever remember seeing daddy laugh?

HARTLEY: No. I don't remember him ever... he was more of a brooder.

HUGO: Brooder, yes. That's what I said.

HARTLEY: He liked to glower.

HUGO: Glower, exactly. I'm glad he's dead. Is that bad?

HARTLEY: No.

Beat.

HUGO: They gave me some money afterwards. The man kept most of it. He said I should use the rest to cheer myself up.

Beat.

HUGO: It's not very much. Here.

He digs into his pocket.

HARTLEY: Keep it.

HUGO: What about –

HARTLEY: Just keep it safe.

HUGO: About the selling. We can put it towards... till the money comes.

HARTLEY: I think that plan's been sidetracked a little.

Beat.

HUGO: They had a cat. There was a cat.

Beat.

HUGO: I can't stop thinking about mummy. Lying down in the garden. Staring up into the sky. That big black hole in the middle of her chest.

HARTLEY: Try and think of something else.

HUGO: Don't you see it when you close your eyes?

HARTLEY: I'm a butcher. I'm used to much worse.

HUGO: I miss her.

HARTLEY: I know.

HUGO: The man's coming back. He'll keep coming back. What are we going to do?

HARTLEY: Try not to panic.

HUGO: He won't leave us alone.

HARTLEY: I want you to look inside yourself like you used to. Look deep inside yourself. What do you feel?

HUGO: Rage.

HARTLEY: Good. That's good.

HUGO: He gave us away, didn't he? Like all his other assets, we've been used to pay off his debts, haven't we? That's why he did it.

Beat.

HUGO: That's why he did it.

HARTLEY: No, he left us the most priceless gift of all.

HUGO: Did he?

HARTLEY: When I came back from my walk, I thought I'd check the bedroom.

HUGO: Did you find anything?

HARTLEY: There's a box by the bed with your name on it. Why don't you go and have a look?

HUGO exits to the bedroom.

Pause.

HUGO re-enters, wild eyed and breathing heavily.

HUGO: He kept it.

HARTLEY: Yes.

HUGO: He kept it, all this time. Can I put it on?

HARTLEY: Not yet.

HUGO: Please Hartley.

HARTLEY: I said not yet. Get some sleep.

HUGO: When?

HARTLEY: Get some sleep.

HUGO: What's in your box?

HARTLEY: You'll see.

HUGO: He kept it. I can't believe he kept it. Hartley. Hartley look at me.

HARTLEY turns to HUGO.

HUGO: I want to play.

HARTLEY: Good night brother.

HUGO nods, smiles, exits to the bedroom.

HARTLEY takes out the prescription and reads it again.

He moves over to the sell box from earlier. He reaches in and takes out a bottle of prescription medication. He reads the label.

TEDDY enters, on the phone. HARTLEY drops the bottle and the prescription.

TEDDY: Oh I know, it was beautiful. He was, wasn't he a little cherub? What a golden boy, eh? I told you I'd found something special.

TEDDY notices HARTLEY. They stare at each other as he talks into the phone.

TEDDY: Yeah, yeah I know. Lovely... His brother's not quite the same. He lacks the grace, and those features. We'll use him. He strikes me as a bit of a work horse. He'll pay his dues in the passage of time... Don't you worry about that, I'll break him in. I'll take care of it... Clarence, sweetheart, get some sleep love. Busy day tomorrow. Okay, night.

He hangs up. HARTLEY holds his gaze. TEDDY strokes his tie.

TEDDY: You missed out on quite a –

HARTLEY: Let me tell you a story about my father. We had a house cat. A big fat ginger one. It didn't have a name, father insisted that we didn't name it. One day, the cat had kittens. Seven of them. It was the most exciting day of our lives. We begged him to let us keep one. As a pet. With a name and everything. To our... astonishment, he agreed to let us keep not one, but all seven. Seven little kittens that were ours to keep, and look after, and love. Maisy, Daisy, Eugene, Francis, Casper, Annabelle and Socks. That's what we called them. Socks had white paws. Like little socks. Annabelle was constantly getting stuck on high ledges. Daisy was very vocal.

TEDDY: Lovely –

HARTLEY: A few weeks later our father took us outside to the bottom of the garden. Said he had something to show us. We thought it might be more presents. Perhaps he'd turned over a new leaf. Waiting for us at the bottom of the garden was a large metal basin full of ice cold water, an empty potato sack, and a basket containing seven kittens.

Beat.

HARTLEY: He stood over us as we drowned them. Maisy, Daisy, Eugene, Francis, Casper, Annabelle and Socks. We took it in turns, our tears popping the bubbles as they rose to the surface. He never told us why he made us do that, and we never asked.

TEDDY: Tenants aren't allowed pets here either. So still no kittens for you I'm afraid.

HARTLEY: To us, searching for an answer, some kind of logic, it always remained an act of mindless cruelty. But of course that was the point.

TEDDY: You look knackered. You should get some sleep. Big day tomorrow. Your turn.

HARTLEY: Let me tell you a story about Hugo. Once, years later in the middle of the night, I woke up and found his bed empty. He's a good sleeper usually, so I was naturally concerned. I checked the whole house, but I couldn't find him anywhere. And it was a very large house. It took a good hour.

By that point I was genuinely scared for him. Finally I ventured out into the fields in my robe with a torch. And you'll never believe what I saw. In the far field, just before the forest, right there in the inky blackness was a figure stood alone. And the figure was Hugo. And you'll never guess what he was doing –

TEDDY: You two are a right pair of freaks, you know that? Proper bloody weirdos. You're not normal. No wonder he kept you behind closed doors your whole life. You should've heard the things the other lads were saying about your brother tonight. They thought he was retarded. And you know what? I kind of did too. You ain't all there, neither of you. He'll be alright, I like him. Just remember I have the power to make your life a fucking nightmare. A real horror show.

Beat.

TEDDY: We had to gag him tonight. On account of the tears. Your daddy would've loved it. Ironic really.

Beat.

TEDDY: I bet you're a squealer. Aren't you?

He squeals like a pig in HARTLEY's face. Laughs.

TEDDY: Find out tomorrow. Hope you're not squeamish.

TEDDY moves to leave, then spins back round to face HARTLEY.

TEDDY: You look nothing like him, you know that? It's like you weren't even related.

Beat.

TEDDY: Night night.

SCENE FOUR

Dawn. TEDDY is awake and alone. He has been crying.

He takes out a small vial of white powder and taps out a bump onto the back of his hand. He snorts it up and rubs his nose.

He starts to cry again. He reaches down and picks up a scarf from a box. He holds it up to his face and inhales the scent. He cries harder into the scarf.

Behind him, HUGO enters. He is wearing a cloak made entirely of sheep's fur, and a hollowed out ram's head over his own.

TEDDY doesn't notice until he hears HUGO's boots clack on the floor.

TEDDY: Urgh! Oh god.

He stifles the scarf away and wipes his eyes. He tries not to face HUGO for a little while.

TEDDY: Is that you? Scared me then. What are you wearing?

Beat.

TEDDY: What are you doing up? You should be getting your beauty sleep.

Beat.

TEDDY: Only been back a few hours. Go and get your head down. What the fuck are you wearing?

Beat.

TEDDY: I can give you something, help you sleep.

He takes out the vial of powder, shakes it.

TEDDY: Listen to me, get back in bed. I don't want you dozing off at all hours tomorrow, alright? I won't have it.

Beat.

TEDDY: Take that fucking thing off will you?

Beat.

TEDDY: What is it, a comfort thing? Looks fucking weird, take it off.

Beat.

TEDDY: Look. Look... I know. Okay? I know it hurts. Believe me, I know. And I know you feel awful right now, nasty. But it gets easier.

He approaches HUGO.

TEDDY: I'm telling you it gets easier. You're scared, I understand that. But I meant it when I said I'd look after you. I will Hugo, I'll take good care of you.

Beat.

TEDDY: It's what he wanted, boy. Do you understand? It's what he wanted. He knew what you'd be good for. Face like yours, you'll have the debts cleared within a year. And after that... well I know you'll wanna stay with me. I know it. Right here with me.

Beat.

TEDDY: Oh Jesus, why did he have to fucking go and do that? He didn't have to do that.

HUGO nods slowly.

TEDDY: You boys didn't know him like I did.

HUGO nods again.

TEDDY: No you didn't! No one knew him like I did!

TEDDY grabs HUGO and shakes him.

TEDDY: Oh God I'm sorry. Oh sweetheart I'm so sorry.

He kneels down by HUGO and tries to hold him.

TEDDY: I promise I'll never do that again. Never.

HUGO pulls himself free and backs away.

TEDDY: Would you take that fucking thing off your head!

Beat.

TEDDY: Now don't be petulant! That's a very unattractive
habit. It'll get you in a lot of trouble. When someone asks
you to do something, you do it, alright? I don't want you
giving any back chat neither, I won't have you being one
of them types. It doesn't suit you. You're well behaved, and
that's what makes you super super special.

Beat.

TEDDY: But listen, we need to do something about the
screaming. I know it was your first night and it's all new
to you but we really need to work on getting that under
control –

HUGO produces a cane and holds it out towards TEDDY.

Beat. TEDDY laughs.

TEDDY: Hello. Where'd that come from? Look at you with
your big stick.

TEDDY looks at the cane.

TEDDY: I remember this stick.

He presses his lips to the end of it.

TEDDY: That cold brass. What did you think of the other boys
tonight? You get on well with them?

Beat.

TEDDY: They're good lads. Girls are a bit funny. Weird accents
and that. We've had some issues, clients who wanna make
conversation. So what are you gonna do with that money?
Eh? Given it any thought?

*He turns again. HUGO is still holding the cane like a bat. TEDDY
laughs again.*

TEDDY: What are you doing?

HUGO tightens his grip around the cane.

TEDDY: Sweetheart, why are you holding that stick?

He takes a step closer.

TEDDY: You're upset aren't you? Look at you, you're upset.

He tuts, takes a step closer.

TEDDY: Come here –

HUGO holds him away with the cane.

TEDDY: What? You gonna hit me? Well, go on then.

TEDDY points to his head.

TEDDY: Go on then! Gimme a whack on me old noggin. Give old Teddy a bop on the head. I said go on then. Hit me!

HUGO does not move.

TEDDY: Thought so. You think I don't know what you're going through? I know, it'll pass. It always does. Everyone prangs out a little bit, their first time. I have to say though this is something else. Usually it's just a few tears –

HUGO pokes him in the throat with the cane. He gags.

TEDDY: Watch it with that bloody thing.

He moves towards him. HUGO pushes the cane into his face, keeping him away.

TEDDY: What the fuck – off me!

He steps back, annoyed.

TEDDY: What's your problem? You little fucking –

He grabs the end of the cane and holds it.

TEDDY: Are you gonna behave yourself?

Pause.

He lets go of the cane. HUGO lowers it.

TEDDY: Good boy.

He moves over to HUGO and pulls off the ram's head.

HUGO: I'm a goatherd. And my brother is a butcher.

HARTLEY emerges from the bedroom dressed in pristine butcher's whites. He is holding a huge shiny knife.

TEDDY feels him at his back, spins round. HUGO raises the cane again.

TEDDY: Oh that's cute. That's really cute. Have you thought this through? Have you? Course you fucking haven't.

HUGO: We're not normal.

He turns to HUGO.

TEDDY: I told you I'd look after you.

HUGO: Maisy, Daisy, Eugene...

TEDDY: You stupid little – I told you it's what he wanted!

HUGO: Francis, Casper, Annabel...

TEDDY: It was his plan. Do you understand?

HUGO: And socks.

TEDDY: You were his gift to me.

HARTLEY: The vast, echoing silence of our family home. The banal ritual of slaughter. The distinct lack of answers to the most natural and human of questions.

HUGO: The isolation.

TEDDY: Fuck are you on about?

HARTLEY: When a cat had kittens...

HUGO: We drowned them.

HARTLEY: When a horse broke its leg...

HUGO: We shot it.

HARTLEY: When a farmhand was injured...

HUGO: We fired them.

HARTLEY: When rival farms had a better year...

HUGO: We burned their crops to the ground.

HARTLEY: When something became worthless, a burden...

HUGO: Cumbersome estate. Conspicuous family name...

TEDDY: I'm giving you one more chance here.

HUGO: It was destroyed.

HARTLEY: A useless old man, dying of Parkinson's disease.

HUGO: A liability to our survival.

HARTLEY: He knew the rules. He knew what was required.

HUGO: They ended up on the fire with the rest of the livestock.

TEDDY: You're wrong. Both of you, you're bloody wrong.

Beat.

HARTLEY: Our personal interaction with others kept minimal.

HUGO: Almost zero.

TEDDY: Look I know it's different up there. On the farm.

HARTLEY: And when someone did try to get close to us...

HUGO: Our father blinded him.

TEDDY: It's all life and death, innit? Kill or be...

HARTLEY: We are untamed to the laws and customs of civilised society.

HUGO: Incapable of emotional connection with another living thing.

TEDDY: But that's not how it works down here, in the real world. There's etiquette, there's...

HARTLEY: We are not human.

TEDDY: I'll teach you. I'll teach you everything you need to know, okay?

HUGO: His sons and heirs.

TEDDY: This is the way it's supposed to work. It's why you're so special. You're pristine. You're untouched.

HUGO nudges him with the cane.

TEDDY: We'll start tomorrow. I'll teach you everything. All the things he never did. It'll be different now. I promise, a new life. Let's have a nap and we can talk it through later, eh? We'll have a good old chat tomorrow.

He takes out his mobile phone and tries to dial a number. HUGO knocks it out of his hand with the cane.

TEDDY: Okay, you don't like the parties. That's fine. We can... we can think of something else. It was probably a bit much, all them people, but we can try you on something else. The pair of you together if that's better for you.

HUGO and HARTLEY approach him from either side.

TEDDY: He left you with nothing. You have nothing. But that's okay, because you have me. You have me.

He holds HUGO's face.

HARTLEY: Exactly.

HUGO pushes his face into TEDDY's. With a feral growl, he bites down into TEDDY's ear. He pulls away, his mouth full of blood.

HARTLEY stabs TEDDY and drags the knife upwards through his guts.

TEDDY collapses behind the sofa. HUGO beats him viciously with the cane.

HARTLEY drags him off into the bedroom. HUGO follows. The door slams.

From the bedroom, the sound of screeching, banging, bones cracking, hacking and laughter.

The sun rises outside.

After a moment, TEDDY's mobile phone rings from behind the sofa.

HARTLEY enters, his whites are soaked in blood. He moves over to the ringing phone.

HARTLEY: Hello? Clarence, I'm so glad you called. I want you to listen very carefully. Your master is dead. I killed him. I am a butcher of some distinction and my brother is a noble goatherd. We're new to the area, and we've come to take over the empire. You belong to us now. All of you. Clarence, calm down.

Clarence, it's very important you listen to me. Clarence, I want you to go out there and tell them that we'll be back in business in no time. I'll take care of the bad meat, my brother Hugo will be in charge of all your livestock... don't worry, you'll recognise him. He'll be wearing your master's face.

HUGO enters, soaked more or less head-to-toe in blood. He is holding TEDDY's heart.

HUGO: Love Heart?

HARTLEY: Yes Huggy Bear?

HUGO: Can we sell this?

HARTLEY: Of course! We can sell everything!

HARTLEY drops the phone and laughs a loud, wild laugh.

They sing as loud as they can.

HARTLEY & HUGO:
In the fair fields of wheat and heather
Fa la la la la la la la la!
Let the children wander free forever
Fa la la la la la la la la!
Keep them plump and well on meat and dairy
Fa la la la la la la la la!
And forevermore may they be merry
Fa la la la la la la la la!

May the song of nature be always in our hearts!
And may our sacks be fat with grain before the winter starts!
And may the sound of birdsong hang so sweetly in the sky!
And may the rain keep wet what's wet, and the sun keep dry what's dry!

HUGO: And so we kneel before our saviour watching from the sky!

A loud, animalistic shriek.

Blackout.